New Testament PRIESTS, Speak Up!

Encouraging Broader Participation in the Lord's Supper

— Mike Stephenson —

Many ECS publications are also available in eBook formats. For more information, visit our website www.ecsministries.org.

New Testament Priests, Speak Up!

Mike Stephenson

Published by:
ECS Ministries
PO Box 1028
Dubuque, IA 52004-1028
phone: (563) 585-2070
email: ecsorders@ecsministries.org
website: www.ecsministries.org

First Edition 2015

ISBN 978-1-59387-229-8

Code: B-NTPSU

Copyright © 2015 ECS Ministries

All Scripture quotations, unless otherwise indicated, are Scripture taken from the NEW AMERICAN STANDARD BIBLE®, Copyright © 1960, 1962, 1963, 1968, 1971, 1972, 1973, 1975, 1977, 1995 by The Lockman Foundation. Used by permission.

All rights reserved. No part of this publication may be reproduced or transmitted in any manner, electronic or mechanical, including photocopy, recording, or any information storage and retrieval system including the Internet without written permission from the publisher. Permission is not needed for brief quotations embodied in critical articles and reviews.

Printed in the United States of America

Contents

Preface 5
A Personal Note 7

Part 1 – The Encouragement Program
   Our Lord's Supper Training Sessions 11

Part 2 – Biblical Reasons to Participate
   1. The Primary Objectives of the Lord's Supper 17
   2. The Priesthood of All Believers 21
   3. Insights from 1 Corinthians 14:26-40 25
   4. Worship and the Lord's Supper 29

Part 3 – Practical Concerns
   5. Why We Often Don't Share 37
   6. Why or When We Shouldn't Share 43
   7. What We Should and Shouldn't Share 47
   8. A Few Words About Delivery 53
   9. How to Follow the Leading of the Holy Spirit 55
   10. How Best to Prepare to Participate 59

Part 4 – Conclusion
   Afterword 65

Addendum A – So What's In It for Women? 67
Addendum B – Session Worksheets 69
Endnotes 77
About the Author 79

Preface

A number of people today are concerned about the meeting where we gather together specifically to remember the Lord Jesus Christ. We call the meeting by different names, using titles such as the Lord's Supper, the breaking of bread, the worship meeting, and the remembrance meeting.

Their concern rests in the fact that, as they see it, participation in the meeting is no longer as fresh, as inspiring, or even as genuine as it used to be or should be. Perhaps they have observed that only a relatively small number of men are willing to participate in the meeting from week to week, often the same men every week. Maybe attendance has dropped off over time, particularly among the young people.

These are valid concerns. So how can they be addressed?

This book is one response. Here the author relates how, through a series of meetings, he and his assembly attempted to help some of the men develop a greater appreciation for the Lord's Supper and a better understanding of how they might participate in it with some regularity. The exact approach and ideas may not suit the situation in your local church perfectly, but hopefully it will stimulate you to consider how you can best address the issues that may exist in your assembly in regard to this most important of meetings.

A Personal Note

I was impressed the very first time I experienced the Lord's Supper as the culmination of a service devoted entirely to worship. Oh, I had observed the Lord's Supper before but always as a brief add-on to the standard 11am Sunday service devoted primarily to teaching. If I recall correctly, that add-on took place about once a quarter at the mainline denominational church I grew up in.

Now, at this early juncture, I should clarify what I mean in my opening statement for those who do not attend what is often referred to as a "Brethren assembly" (or church). The typical Brethren assembly of believers observes the Lord's Supper every week. Normally, the passing of the bread and the cup takes place at or near the end of a period of time, usually an hour, devoted to worshiping the Lord God and remembering what Christ accomplished for us through His death and resurrection. In many assemblies it is an unplanned and unstructured meeting. Instead of being led by a select group of church professionals in front of the congregation, the meeting is conducted by various men, not necessarily church leaders, who stand up spontaneously from right where they are sitting and participate, one at a time, ideally according to how the Holy Spirit leads them. They may, for example, pray, read a passage of Scripture, make some comments on that passage, or suggest a hymn to be sung.

My first experience of the Lord's Supper as I have just described it took place shortly after I arrived for nine months of missionary training at the facility of an organization known then as Literature Crusades (now called International Teams). We gathered on that first Sunday morning in a large meeting room, and I watched joyfully as one young man after another stood up to share with us his thoughts about God our Father and/or about our Lord and Savior, Jesus Christ. I have been involved in Brethren assemblies ever since, and one of the main reasons is because of this very uplifting observance of the Lord's Supper, which I have found nowhere else.

Of course, this is not to say that this type of meeting is always perfect in every way. Indeed, I have often wondered why the Lord's Supper many times does not seem to be as spontaneous as we would like it to be. In particular, why is it that in many assemblies the same relatively small number of men carry the bulk of the supposedly spontaneous sharing week in and week out? At least that's what I had observed until I started attending a national assembly in a Middle Eastern country where I lived and worked as an English teacher for over eight years. I discovered that in that assembly, they conducted the Lord's Supper quite differently than how we do it in the United States. They would start out by singing hymns for about twenty minutes. Then they would move into a time of prayer, and in a congregation which included about twenty-five to thirty adult and teenage males, the majority of them would take their turn praising God and glorifying Jesus for what He had done for them on the cross. After that, the elements would be passed around, and finally, one brother would go up to the pulpit to deliver a message. What caught my attention the most was how so many of the men participated in the meeting every single week. And I thought to myself, if they can get most of the men to feel the liberty to participate in the breaking of bread on a regular basis, why can't we do so here in the United States?

That experience among believers in the Middle East is what prompted me to offer some training classes for men in my home assembly, to teach them what and how to share in the Lord's Supper and to help them overcome their reticence to do so. The schedule we followed involved a weekly evening meeting for ten weeks. We had a great time looking at what the Scriptures teach about the Lord's Supper and discussing practical aspects related to participation in this meeting. It was beneficial for us all to think about why we do what we do in the Lord's Supper in more depth than we ever had before. Shortly after I concluded those sessions, I was contacted by ECS Ministries about the possibility of my putting what I had taught into words to be published as a help to others, the result of which you have before you.

–Mike Stephenson, 2015

PART 1
THE ENCOURAGEMENT PROGRAM

New Testament Priests, Speak Up!

Our Lord's Supper Training Sessions

In the previous pages I alluded to a series of training sessions on the Lord's Supper that I offered for a group of interested men in the assembly I attend. The idea of training sessions for participation in the Lord's Supper may sound unusual or even inappropriate to some. After all, isn't participation in this meeting supposed to be spontaneous and Spirit-led? Yes, that's true. But it's also true that some who attend the Lord's Supper don't always have a clear understanding of what we're trying to accomplish in that meeting, and others who may have that understanding have misconceptions about who can vocally contribute to the meeting and how that should be done. Thus the goal of the sessions was to correctly inform the attendees and to encourage them to regularly share in the meeting.

The schedule we made was to meet together once a week for ten weeks, for an hour and a half each time. Counting myself, there were nine of us involved. Several of the men were not from a Brethren assembly background, and I was particularly happy that they had decided to join in with us. I asked that those who attended would commit themselves to come to every session if at all possible, and attendance was outstanding, which improved the quality of the sessions.

The first four sessions were devoted to covering the contents of this book, which at that time constituted just my own notes that I had written out in a notebook.

Session 1 – We looked at all the Bible passages that specifically focus on or refer to the Lord's Supper (see chapter 1 of this book).

Session 2 – We went through other portions of Scripture that, though they don't mention the Lord's Supper, nevertheless greatly influence how we conduct the meeting (see chapters 2–4). I asked a variety of questions to get everyone involved and thinking about the implications of the Bible passages we were reading.

Sessions 3 and 4 – In these sessions we worked through the various practical issues of vocal participation in the Lord's Supper covered in chapters 5–10.

Beginning with the fifth session, there was some homework to do in order to be ready for that week's session. At that point, the sessions became more student than teacher centered.

Session 5 – For this session, the attendees were asked to look at Psalm 103 and Ephesians 2:1-10 and pick out from each passage a phrase or a verse or two that focuses on who the Lord is and/or how He has redeemed us. I also had them take home a copy of the two hymnbooks we use in our remembrance meeting. I picked out a variety of hymns for the men to look over and determine which are most appropriate for the meeting and which are less so and why. I had them point out particular phrases in each hymn to support their opinions.

Session 6 – This session was similar to the fifth one except that, instead of me assigning Bible passages for them to read, I asked them to choose a Bible passage themselves and be prepared to point out thoughts from the passage that could be used in the Lord's Supper and thoughts from the passage that might not be as appropriate. They were also expected to pick out both a suitable and a less suitable hymn from each hymnbook and to explain the reasoning behind their choices.

Sessions 7 to 10 – The last four sessions were devoted to conducting "practice" Lord's Supper meetings. My feeling was that, more than anything, most of them simply needed some nonthreatening opportunities to practice sharing in public. I will readily admit that these practice sessions lacked to some degree in the area of spontaneity because one of the guidelines for these meetings was that each of them was expected to participate in one of the following three ways:

✓ by praying
✓ by reading and commenting on a Scripture passage
✓ by commenting on a hymn to be sung.

Actually, I asked them all to come prepared to share from a Bible passage even though they would probably not all have the opportunity to do so. I pointed out that while these practice sessions would be a bit more restrictive than a regular Sunday Lord's Supper meeting, we could nevertheless look to the Holy Spirit, waiting upon Him for His leading as to the right time for each of us to participate vocally in each meeting. I requested that whoever gave thanks in prayer for the bread or the cup would also be the one to get up and serve that particular element to the rest of us. In addition, I reminded them not to be unnerved by a little silence and to feel free to share more than once if they felt led to. Since we met on a weeknight, I also encouraged them to consider sharing thoughts that had come to them during the previous Sunday's breaking of bread. As there were only nine of us in these practice sessions, they usually lasted no more than about forty-five minutes. At the end of each session, I would give them some brief feedback, mostly positive, as to the appropriateness of their contributions and the effectiveness of their delivery.

Beginning with the fifth session, I encouraged all of us to pay close attention to the previous Sunday's Lord's Supper, even taking notes on the meeting, to see if we could determine the theme or themes of that meeting. At the next session, we would spend a few minutes comparing notes to determine what we thought the Spirit was communicating to us in that Lord's Supper. At times, we detected a clear, singular theme, but at other times, there seemed to be multiple themes.

Now, what if you don't have a group the size of what we had for these practice sessions? What if you have only two or three men? You could still have them prepare some comments on a Bible passage to share before the group, pick out a hymn that you would sing together, and then pray in response to the thoughts contained in those Bible passages and hymns. They'd still be getting some practice determining what kinds of remarks fit at the Lord's Supper and sharing audibly in front of others. In fact, the second time I took a group of men through this material, there were only four or five of us, so I required them to participate in all three ways in each of these practice sessions.

Session 10 – We made the tenth and final session a bit special. We decided to have a potluck meal that night before the practice Lord's Supper. All but one of the men in the group were married, so I asked them to bring their wives and children to this final session. The one single man invited a family that he was close to as his guests. We also invited one of our elders and his family to this event. In my mind, the primary reason for this was to give the men in the group an opportunity to share publicly before an even larger group, yet one in which they should feel reasonably comfortable. In all, there were about thirty of us present that night. After a wonderful meal together, reminiscent of how the first century Christians must have done it, we then moved upstairs to the room where we hold our worship meeting on Sunday. After I made a few comments of encouragement and challenge to the men who had attended for the previous nine weeks, we had our final practice Lord's Supper meeting. All of us were expected to participate, and the other two men who were present were invited to take part as well if they wanted to. As I recall, every man in attendance did participate, and we enjoyed a nice time of remembering and worshiping the Lord together. It was a fitting end to our series of training sessions.

For your convenience, some worksheets have been provided in Addendum B for use in taking notes and preparing for your practical assignments.

PART 2
BIBLICAL REASONS TO PARTICIPATE

– NEW – TESTAMENT PRIESTS, Speak Up!

Chapter 1

The Primary Objectives of the Lord's Supper

Obviously, anyone who would participate in the Lord's Supper vocally must have a clear understanding of why we hold this meeting in the first place and what we're trying to accomplish in it. At the very first breaking of bread, introduced by Jesus Himself, our Lord both implies and directly states the reasons for this meeting.

> *While they were eating, Jesus took some bread, and after a blessing, He broke it and gave it to the disciples, and said, "Take, eat; this is My body." And when He had taken a cup and given thanks, He gave it to them saying, "Drink from it, all of you; for this is My blood of the covenant, which is poured out for many for forgiveness of sins." (Matt. 26:26-28)*

Notice that these are commands of our Lord, not merely suggestions. Thus, participation in this observance is our duty as His followers, and an indispensible component of church life and practice.

In these commands, Jesus was and is calling all who would be His disciples to identify with Him by willingly receiving these basic elements. This identification with our Lord seems to be at least one of the implications of 1 Corinthians 10:16, where Paul writes,

> *Is not the cup of blessing which we bless a sharing in the blood of Christ? Is not the bread which we break a sharing in the body of Christ?*

Moreover, Jesus' intentional gathering of His disciples both to celebrate the Passover and to introduce this new ordinance (Luke 22:7-20) gives weight to the conclusion that this new observance must be performed along with a group of other believers. It's a public event, not a private one. This is confirmed by the fact that wherever the breaking of bread is mentioned in the Scriptures in addition to the Gospels (Matt. 26:26-30; Mark 14:22-26; Luke 22:14-20), we find that it is always a group activity (Acts 2:42, 46; 20:7; 1 Cor. 11:17-20, 33-34). This is also another strong implication of 1 Corinthians 10:16, quoted above, as well as of verse 17: "Since there is one bread, we who are many are one body; for we all partake of the one bread." We believers celebrate and share in the Lord's Supper together, and that should unite us not just in spirit but in practice as well.

It is further recorded in Luke 22:19-20 that Jesus proclaimed,

> *"This is My body which is given for you; do this in remembrance of Me. . . This cup which is poured out for you is the new covenant in My blood."*

Jesus commands us not simply to partake of the elements but also to remember Him as we do that. What are we remembering about Him as we participate in this meeting? We're remembering that it's through His tortured body, His shed blood, and His ultimate death that we have complete forgiveness of our sins, as we've already seen in Matthew 26:28. In addition, we enjoy a new, eternal relationship with God based on a new covenant with Him through Christ's sacrifice. William Kelly, in his book entitled *Lectures on the Church of God,* states it very simply, "To take the Supper in remembrance of the Lord, and thus show forth His death, is what gathers us together as our prime desire."[1]

In my reading on this subject of the Lord's Supper, I came across the suggestion more than once that when Jesus referred to "the new covenant," He primarily had in mind the new covenant that God laid out for His people Israel in Jeremiah 31:31-34, an agreement with Israel that God will implement fully during the millennium. Nevertheless, at the same time, all of us who are now in Christ's body, the church, whether Jew or Gentile, are already enjoying many of the wonderful benefits outlined in that new covenant. To begin with, we have clearly entered into a new relationship with God through Christ (Eph. 2). We Christians can confidently say that God is our God and we are His people (Jer. 31:33; Rom. 8:14-17). We can say that we all know Him (v. 34; John 17:3) and that He has forgiven us of our many sins against Him (v. 34; Luke 24:45-47). We can even say that, as we draw nearer to God and become more familiar with His Word and practice it more faithfully, the conscience that God has given to each one of us (Rom. 2:14-16) is reworked to such an extent that we become people on whose hearts God's law is written (v. 33; Titus 2:11-14). The new covenant or testament that is currently in effect for those in the church is referred to in 2 Corinthians 3:5-6 and in several passages in Hebrews (7:22-28; 8:6; 9:11-15; 12:24; 13:20).

Surely the Lord Jesus must have had an immediate as well as a future fulfillment of "the new covenant" in mind when He spoke those words. As we remember and "proclaim the Lord's death" (1 Cor. 11:26), we rejoice in the fact that these and many other benefits are inextricably tied to His sacrificial death in our place.

Of course, the timing of that very first breaking of bread service was no coincidence. Jesus chose to introduce this observance on the very night before His crucifixion. According to Luke 22:15, it also took place on the Passover, that major Jewish holiday in which Jews remember how God spared their firstborn children in Egypt as they obeyed Him by offering a lamb as a sacrifice in place of their firstborn, putting the blood of that lamb around the door of each Jewish home for the angel of death to see and pass over (Exodus 12). In similar fashion, as we take the bread and drink the cup, we remember that Jesus became the sacrificial Lamb given by the Father for the salvation of everyone who has genuine faith in His Son.

Finally, in 1 Corinthians 11, the apostle Paul, after recounting the words which Jesus uttered at that inaugural Lord's Supper, follows those words with an important comment about this observance. In verse 26 he writes, "For as often as you eat this bread and drink the cup, you proclaim the Lord's death until He comes." To me, this brief statement is one that's just brimming over with hope. Our proclamation, our announcement, is not primarily one of mourning over the fact that our sins led directly to the death of our sinless

Savior, though that is undeniably true. Rather, we're proclaiming the power of His death over our sin and the spiritual liberation that is ours through His sacrifice. Moreover, we're continually looking forward to the consummation of our salvation when He triumphantly returns.

In his book *New Testament Church Principles*, Arthur Clarke says of the Lord's Supper:

> The occasion is not simply one of retrospection but is an act of celebration and, be it noted, not of His death only but of Him. . . . Ours is a joyful celebration of One who, having accomplished the atoning work of the cross, rose triumphant from the tomb and ascended to the right hand of God. He is commemorated, therefore, not as a long-absent One so much as One who ever lives and is present according to His gracious promise.[2]

So there you have it. When we gather together for the Lord's Supper, it is to obey Him, to identify with Him, to stand united in Him, to remember Him, and to joyfully proclaim the life-changing power of His work on behalf of all who would put their trust in Him. Anyone who would stand up and lead out in worship during the Lord's Supper must keep these objectives in mind, and in particular, the Lord's specific command, "Do this in remembrance of Me."

CHAPTER 2

The Priesthood of All Believers

The critical passage of Scripture in regard to the priesthood of all believers in Christ is certainly 1 Peter 2:4-10. In this passage, addressed to all believers, the Lord through Peter proclaims that we "are being built up as a spiritual house for a holy priesthood" and that we are "a royal priesthood." The same point is made in Revelation 1:6 and 5:10. Well, what function did the priests of the Old Testament serve among the people of Israel? They were the only ones among the people of Israel who were permitted into the tabernacle (or later, the temple) to perform the various acts of worship of God on behalf of the people (Ex. 27:20-1; 28:1-3; 29:44; 30:17-21; 40:12-15). Furthermore, any sacrifices or offerings that the people desired to present to the Lord had to be brought to the priests, who would serve as intermediaries between the people and God (Lev. 4:27-35; 16:29-34; 23:9-11). Thus the priests represented and led the people when they wanted to approach and worship God. Their ministry was also to a large degree public, performed before the people of God.

Now, we believers in New Testament times are also called to be priests, but not just some of us—all of us! Returning to our passage in 1 Peter 2, we read that we are all holy priests whose privilege it is to "offer up spiritual sacrifices acceptable to God through Jesus Christ" and to "proclaim the excellencies of Him who has called you out of darkness into His marvelous light." As those who are trusting in Christ as the ultimate sacrifice for our sins, once for all time, we no longer need to offer animal sacrifices. Thus, our "spiritual sacrifices" would include such things as mentioned in Hebrews 13:15: "Through

Him then, let us continually offer up a sacrifice of praise to God, that is, the fruit of lips that give thanks to His name." Such acts of worship can be performed either audibly or silently as we gather together to remember the Lord.

Furthermore, if we are all priests, then it follows that there is no part of the Lord's Supper in which we are not qualified to take the lead. This would include praying for and distributing the elements—the bread and the cup. You do not have to be an ordained minister, elder, deacon, or some other church official in order to pray for the elements or to pass them to the congregation of worshipers. Kelly has this to say about the matter:

> Yet supposing that the administration, as men call it, of the Supper of the Lord is committed to a real minister of Christ, or to all who are His ministers, as the exclusive prerogative of such as minister only . . . under any and all circumstances, it is a human invention, not only without the authority of Christ, but decidedly contrary to the doctrine and facts recorded in scripture. I admit to ministry most fully; but the Lord's Supper has no connexion with it. Make it a necessary function of those that rule to administer the bread and wine, and it bears not even an outward resemblance to the Lord's Supper. It becomes a sacrament, not His Supper; a manifest innovation, a decided and complete departure from what the Lord has laid down in His word. The very idea of a person standing apart and claiming to administer it as a right alters and ruins the Supper of the Lord. That Supper, according to scripture, leaves no room for the display of human importance in the pretensions of a clergy; least of all when the apostles were on earth. Blessed and honoured of God as these were at the celebration of the Lord's Supper, they were there in His presence as souls that were saved from sin and its judgment by the Lord's death.[3]

Though Kelly and the others who were instrumental in the launching of the Brethren assembly movement back in the early part of the 19th century may not have been the very first to understand and practice the priesthood of all believers, it was still a radical conclusion for their time. It has been a liberating conclusion for us ever since.

Another related thought is this: it was supremely important for the Old Testament priests to be ceremonially clean and holy before they engaged in any acts of worship of God (Ex. 28:40-43; 29:19-21; 30:17-21; Lev. 8, 16, 21, 22:9). Just like the apostles, we who are in Christ have all been justified and purified by the sacrifice and shed blood of Christ. In and through Christ, we have all essentially become like Him—fully acceptable to God. Thus, if we are all priests and all perpetually clean before God—not just ceremonially but in reality— we are all equally qualified and privileged to lead the congregation in worship.

Finally, in the Old Testament there was always a high priest among the priests who alone was permitted to enter the Holy of Holies in the tabernacle or temple only once a year to offer the atoning sacrifice for himself, for the other priests and for all the people of Israel (Lev. 16; Heb. 9:6-7). Today, we New Testament priests have our own eternal High Priest who, having offered Himself as our redeeming sacrifice, continually represents us before God—the very One we seek to remember and honor during the breaking of bread, the Lord Jesus Christ (Heb. 2:17-18; 4:14-16; 7:23-28; 10:19-22). As a result, we are exhorted, "Since we have confidence to enter the holy place by the blood of Jesus . . . let us draw near with a sincere heart in full assurance of faith . . ." (Heb. 10:19, 22).

Well, then, what are we waiting for? Like no other meeting, the Lord's Supper as we conduct it in assembly circles provides us priests the opportunity to confidently approach the Lord in public worship and to lead God's people in that worship.

Chapter 3

Insights from 1 Corinthians 14:26-40

Another very important passage that has significant bearing upon how the Lord's Supper is conducted is 1 Corinthians 14:26-40. Leon Morris, in his commentary on this passage, says, "This little paragraph is very important as giving us the most intimate glimpse we have of the early church at worship."[4] While 1 Corinthians 11:17-34 is the passage that pertains directly to the Lord's Supper, this passage in chapter 14 describes a meeting of the church that is obviously open and unstructured, and in that way it is similar to the way we conduct our remembrance meetings today. Thus the principles of meeting that Paul lays out here undoubtedly apply as we observe the Lord's Supper in our own times.

One of the strongest impressions I came away with after looking at this passage more closely was the apparent eagerness of all of the Corinthian believers to participate vocally in their meetings. In verse 26, Paul writes, "When you assemble, *each one* has a psalm, has a teaching, has a revelation, has a tongue, has an interpretation" (emphasis added). In verse 27, when Paul addresses those who speak in tongues in the meeting, he instructs them to do so "each in turn" as opposed, I assume, to several or all at once. In verses 30-31, Paul adds, "But if a revelation is made to another who is seated, the first one must keep silent. For you can all prophesy one by one . . ." Basically, the Corinthian believers were so eager to share publicly in their meetings that Paul felt they needed to be restrained and regulated.

For that reason, Paul provides them with some general guidelines of conduct for their worship. He exhorts them, "All things must be done properly and in an orderly manner" (v. 40), "For God is not a God of confusion but of peace" (v. 33). In other words, any public meeting must be conducted in a controlled and orderly way, even a meeting as spontaneous as the type referred to in this passage. As we saw in the previous paragraph, Paul's direction for an orderly meeting in the Corinthian context was that they participate in the meeting "each in turn" and "one by one."

A second guideline is this: the edification of everyone present in the meeting must always be one of the primary goals. So Paul says simply, "Let all things be done for edification . . . so that all may learn and all may be exhorted" (vv. 26, 31). And while the breaking of bread as we in the assemblies practice it today is not intended to be a time of teaching and exhortation, those of us who lead out in worship must remember that we're worshiping in a public setting, and so we must keep our human listeners in mind as well as the Lord, whom we are primarily either addressing or honoring as we speak.

At this point, we come to the most controversial verses in this passage: verses 34-35. In these two verses, Paul commands:

> *The women are to keep silent in the churches, for they are not permitted to speak, but are to subject themselves, just as the Law also says. And if they desire to learn anything, let them ask their own husbands at home, for it is improper for a woman to speak in church.*

Now, while I am aware of arguments which propose that this passage need not be enforced in today's churches—arguments based on the radical cultural differences between our current Western cultures and those of Paul's day—I believe that it's equally valid, even preferable, to take these verses at face value, however unpopular that stance may be in our Western societies. And let's not forget that among Christians in most non-Western cultures even today, this teaching of Paul would not be viewed as unusual or hard to accept. Paul's statements here seem to be quite categorical and are further supported by another strong command of Paul in 1 Timothy 2:8, 11-12:

> *Therefore I want the men in every place to pray, lifting up holy hands, without wrath and dissension. . . . A woman must quietly receive instruction with entire submissiveness. But I do not allow a woman to teach or exercise authority over a man, but to remain quiet.*

My interest in seeing these passages taken at face value and practiced accordingly in our assemblies has nothing to do with any desire of mine to subjugate women. In fact, if the decision were up to me, I might well push for women to have a greater public voice in our churches since I know a number of women who are spiritually mature and would have profound things to share with us. But the decision is not mine, nor even Paul's. In fact, Paul writes in 1 Corinthians 14:37, "If anyone thinks he is a prophet or spiritual, let him recognize that the things which I write to you *are the Lord's commandment*" (emphasis added).

I made the point in the previous chapter that all believers are priests, and that would include women as well as men. However, based on the passages just quoted above, I must conclude that the Lord has stipulated that all female priests should refrain from participating vocally in the public meetings of the church, especially if such comments involve anything resembling authoritative teaching. Again, the Lord's Supper as practiced in most assemblies is expressly not a meeting for teaching or exhortation. Still, as various men stand up to worship the Lord by reading from God's Word, expounding upon it, praying, or suggesting a hymn to be sung, teaching *does* take place, if simply as a by-product of the worship of God and the remembrance of Christ, the primary activities of the meeting. This is a point well made by David Glock in his booklet entitled *Our Reason To Be: The Centrality of the Lord's Supper in the Life of the Assembly*:

> Over the years I have concluded that the best theology we teach is not from the pulpit, but from the Breaking of Bread. There we learn about the Godhead and the attributes of deity. There we learn about the person and work of Christ. There we learn about the sinfulness of man. There we learn about our great salvation. There we learn about the coming of Christ. There we learn the vocabulary of the Bible: grace,

mercy, redemption, propitiation, reconciliation, atonement, etc. . . . The theology lessons are not theoretical; they are in the mode of worship. The participants are not professionals trained for worship. . . . They are ordinary Christians who through participation in the worship meeting have come to understand and love the cardinal doctrines of the Bible. Regular participation in the Lord's Supper develops an instinct for correct theology. The Breaking of Bread, properly practiced, produces theologians. The remembrance of the Lord Jesus Christ in an open, participative meeting is a safeguard against doctrinal error.[5]

I have quoted Mr. Glock at length to emphasize that authoritative, doctrinal teaching does indeed occur routinely during the Lord's Supper. Therefore, such a meeting is not an appropriate forum for our female priests to be participating in audibly.

Undoubtedly, this all may seem rather negative and oppressive to some, yet I believe that there are a couple of real positives that can come out of this. First of all, if roughly half of any given congregation is expected to remain silent throughout the breaking of bread, then that definitely heightens the responsibility for those who can speak—all the male believers—to be willing to lead out in worship. Obviously, if many of the men are unwilling to speak publicly, the number of people participating vocally will be quite limited. Furthermore, if only the men can speak, this certainly encourages them all the more to be the spiritual leaders in the home and in the assembly as the Scriptures call Christian men to be. And if women, who have been proven scientifically to be much more verbal than men, were allowed to take part audibly, can you imagine how rarely many men would actually share?

So, men, let's accept this challenge and start participating vocally in the Lord's Supper. It's both our privilege and our responsibility. Indeed, how many of us come to the Lord's Supper each week with the same eagerness to stand and proclaim publicly the wonders of our God and Savior that the Corinthian believers demonstrated?

CHAPTER 4

Worship and the Lord's Supper

In an earlier chapter I pointed out the primary reasons why we observe the Lord's Supper—to identify with Christ, to remember Him, and to proclaim the power and wonder of His work on our behalf. These things we do in the breaking of bread as we conduct it in Brethren assemblies. However, aren't these same purposes accomplished by other evangelical churches and denominations that typically observe the Lord's Supper as an add-on to the main preaching service at 11am on Sunday? After all, the original Lord's Supper was an insertion by Christ into the Passover meal He shared with His disciples (Matt. 26:17-30). In Acts 20:7, it appears that the breaking of bread was part of a larger meeting, the bulk of which was devoted to a time of teaching by Paul. In 1 Corinthians 11:17-34, it seems that the breaking of bread was preceded by an actual meal that the believers enjoyed together, however inequitably.

In other words, is there any real Scriptural support for the custom in assembly circles of having a full and separate worship meeting which concludes with the passing of the bread and the cup? In my study of the Scriptures, I don't see any. In reality, much of what we in the assemblies do during the meeting we label the Lord's Supper is largely tradition, including the practice of devoting an entire meeting to the observance.

So why do we who attend Brethren assemblies insist on maintaining this tradition of reserving the Lord's Supper as the climax of a full meeting of spontaneous worship of the Lord? Well, to begin with, it helps to ensure that we spend some time each week actually worshiping the Lord. Much of what happens in other meetings of the church consists of the believers being taught and exhorted from God's Word or believers petitioning God for various needs or believers being informed about what's happening in evangelism or on the mission field. These are all fine activities, but they are not worship in the narrow and primary sense of that word, meaning to give praise, thanks, honor, adoration, and glory to God for who He is and what He has done. All too often, Christians spend far too little time in true worship of God, allowing these other spiritual activities to crowd out time for worship. By devoting a whole meeting to the worship of the Father and the Son, this problem is addressed and remedied.

Assigning an entire weekly meeting of the assembly for such worship also emphasizes the fact that the Lord's Supper is a central and crucial aspect of church life, not a peripheral one which can be hastily attended to on an infrequent basis. Furthermore, if the breaking of bread is tacked onto the regular teaching service, there's a greater likelihood that unbelievers will be present, partake of the elements, and go away with the mistaken idea that they are somehow better off spiritually for having done so. Finally, since the other weekly meetings of the assembly are often led by just a few men, a full, spontaneous worship meeting provides much more of an opportunity for the many male priests in the meeting to actually function as such by leading out in worship.

In his book *Worship, The Christian's Highest Occupation*, A. P. Gibbs makes an outstanding observation. Under the subtitle, "As to the importance of worship," he continues:

> This is indicated by the words: "The Father seeketh such to worship Him" [John 4:23] . . . The importance of worship is sensed by the fact that the occupation of the Father is to seek for worshippers, who shall worship Him in Spirit and in truth. What a tremendous thought this is! "The high and lofty One, Who inhabits eternity," not only condescends to notice a humble believer, but actually desires his sincere worship and seeks for it from him![6]

Indeed, throughout the Scriptures, God's people are called to worship the Lord, and that is regarded as an act of utmost importance. Psalm 69:30-31 reads, "I will praise the name of God with song and magnify Him with thanksgiving. And it will please the LORD better than an ox or a young bull with horns and hoofs."

Psalm 99:1-5 exhorts us as follows:

> *The LORD reigns, let the peoples tremble; He is enthroned above the cherubim, let the earth shake! The LORD is great in Zion, and He is exalted above all the peoples. Let them praise Your great and awesome name; holy is He. The strength of the King loves justice; You have established equity; You have executed justice and righteousness in Jacob. Exalt the LORD our God, and worship at His footstool; holy is He.*

To these two passages we can add the three wonderful scenes of worship we find described in Revelation 5:11-14, 7:9-17, and 19:1-7. Note that these worship scenes take place in heaven, where, I have no doubt, they know exactly what they are doing in the area of worship. As I read those passages, I get a strong sense of the joy, the enthusiasm, and the eagerness with which the various beings in heaven vocally join in the worship of God as well as the importance they place on it. You will notice that it's even a loud affair, very possibly similar to the excitement and level of noise you'd experience at a major sports event. The residents of heaven are not concerned about disturbing anyone with their boisterous worship because everybody is joining in just as enthusiastically. They are absolutely captivated, not distracted by anything from marveling at and glorifying the Lord.

And why not? After all, who or what can compare to God (Ps. 89:5-8; Isa. 40:18-26)? We all owe our very existence to Him, our Creator. He's the most exciting, interesting, stimulating, and awe-inspiring Being in the entire universe. He is perfect, flawless, and absolutely holy. He is the source of all that is good. Were it not for His gracious redemption of us through Christ, we would all be hopelessly and eternally lost. He is completely sovereign over His creation and will judge every human being at the end of time. He will provide for those who choose to worship Him an ideal living environment for all of eternity. This is the One of whom it is written:

> *Now to Him who is able to do far more abundantly beyond all that we ask or think, according to the power that works within us, to Him be the glory in the church and in Christ Jesus to all generations forever and ever. Amen. (Eph. 3:20-21)*

Now, as for our own worship here on earth, Gibbs asserts, "There is no spot nearer heaven than when the united worship of an assembly of Christians ascends, like fragrant incense, before the face of God."[7] Is that our sense of it when we gather to worship God and remember our Savior? Do we do our part to make it so? Do we come to this meeting full of a strong desire to please the Lord, full of an irrepressible joy in knowing God and coming into His presence, a joy that compels us to speak out and praise Him? It's not just the inhabitants of heaven who feel that way; the first century believers demonstrated a similar eagerness to worship and remember Him. Thus we can do the same today.

We might further note about those three passages in Revelation that such worship of the Lord, though it can be done individually and privately, is apparently better done as believers gather together for just that reason. In heaven, worshipers come together in huge numbers to give glory to God. The same idea of corporate worship, of worshiping God before other believers, is found in Psalm 22:22-25:

> *I will tell of Your name to my brethren; in the midst of the assembly I will praise You. You who fear the LORD, praise Him; all you descendants of Jacob, glorify Him, and stand in awe of Him, all you descendants of Israel. For He has not despised nor abhorred the affliction of the afflicted; nor has He hidden His face from him; but when he cried to Him for help, He heard. From You comes my praise in the great assembly; I shall pay my vows before those who fear Him.*

We see the exhortation to corporate worship in Psalm 34:3 as well: "O magnify the LORD with me, and let us exalt His name together." We see it also in Psalm 35:18, where we read, "I will give You thanks in the great congregation; I will praise You among a mighty throng."

We see it yet again in Psalm 111:1: "Praise the Lord! I will give thanks to the Lord with all my heart, in the company of the upright and in the assembly."

Finally, can we imagine any better time to partake of the Lord's Supper than after an uplifting time of corporate worship? Is there anything more natural, spiritually speaking, having reflected upon what God has done for us through Christ, than to respond to Him in worship? Clarke makes a helpful observation:

> The basis of worship is an experience of redemption. . . . We note that in the typical order [in the Old Testament] qualified priests were called . . . cleansed . . . clothed . . . and consecrated, set apart for holy service first by the application of blood. . . . Every detail has its spiritual counterpart in the Christian priesthood. In Hebrew to consecrate means literally "to fill the hands." As sinners we approach God with empty hands but as worshippers it is otherwise . . .[8]

Yes, it must be admitted that the way we in the Brethren assemblies observe the Lord's Supper—as a full and separate worship meeting—is largely a tradition. But it's a very good tradition because it promotes true worship of God by those who should be expected to worship Him. In this regard, Glock comes to a very interesting conclusion:

> Yet, in the area of the priesthood of all believers in corporate worship, the Assembly movement has not yet delivered to the evangelical world the privilege of the unique worship that we have enjoyed since the early 1800s. It is the premise of this booklet that this is our reason to exist as a movement.[9]

As has been pointed out in this chapter, the Lord is actually seeking those who would worship Him and who would do so sincerely, enthusiastically and unashamedly in a public context. Will you be one of those worshipers? Can He count on you?

PART 3
PRACTICAL CONCERNS

New Testament Priests, Speak Up!

Chapter 5

Why We Often Don't Share

So far, we have essentially been considering a number of reasons why we male priests should embrace our responsibility and privilege to participate audibly in the Lord's Supper. So why is it that, despite a variety of good reasons to take part, many of us choose rarely if ever to lead out in the breaking of bread? Well, I'm sure the list of excuses is long, and I'll undoubtedly miss some of them, but I'd like for us to look at a few of them at least.

I would suppose that the most prevalent reason for men not sharing in the Lord's Supper is that they're afraid to. They're overly concerned about how they will look or sound, what others will think of them, whether they'll say exactly the right thing, whether they'll go blank as soon as they stand up, and so on. By nature, I myself am a reserved person, and though I have shared in the breaking of bread many times, I find that I still get a bit nervous before I stand up, and sometimes even while I'm sharing. Nevertheless, the Lord has helped me to overcome my natural timidity through the means I'm about to mention.

I think the primary way to combat this obstacle to sharing is for us to stop focusing so much on ourselves and to realize that our leading out in worship is something we're doing to please the Lord, not to please ourselves or others. Furthermore, if we keep what we share brief and simple, we're far less likely to forget part or all of what we intended to say. And let's face it—feeling comfortable when we speak before a group of people tends to come only as we gain experience doing it. That's all the more reason for those just beginning to participate audibly in the breaking of bread to keep their comments or prayers short and uncomplicated.

We may worry about what our wives, our parents, or our friends in the assembly think when we share. In many cases those people may be the most excited to hear us participate. At the very least, I think that many in the meeting would find it refreshing to hear yet another person lead the group in worship.

Another reason someone may not share is because he doesn't want to draw attention to himself. After all, the point of the Lord's Supper is to focus our attention on Christ. Yet, we have already seen that the Lord wants us to lead out in worship, and if we go about it with the right attitude, we will be drawing attention to Christ, not to ourselves. And, obviously, if every man in the meeting chose not to participate audibly for this reason, there would be no meeting, and no attention would be directed to our Lord!

Yet others may conclude that they can't share in public because they see themselves as hypocrites—their walk with the Lord is not strong enough. Well, if we ruled out all hypocrites, few if any believers would be left to take the lead in worship since we're all hypocrites to one degree or another. Remember that the Lord's Supper is a meeting designed for redeemed sinners to reflect upon how the Lord has done for them what they were incapable of doing for themselves. It's a time for all redeemed sinners to thank and praise the Lord for how He has served and rescued them, not a time for a handful of "super-saints" to display how well they're doing spiritually.

Another reason why some may not share is that they can't think of anything new or different to say than what they've already heard many times before in previous meetings. Yet we're gathered in the Lord's name not to invent clever new ideas but to remember who Jesus is and what He's done for us—two things that are established and will not change. The following comment by Kelly addresses both this and the previous objection to sharing:

> I cannot think the assembly of God is the right place for any man to stand up and show his superior wisdom in; on the contrary, therein, above all occasions, is the place for the greatest to show his littleness before God.[10]

Indeed, in 1 Corinthians 1:17-2:5 the apostle Paul goes to great lengths to make this very point about his preaching of the gospel, which he delivered "not in cleverness of speech." He wrote, "I did not come with superiority of speech or of wisdom . . . And my message and my preaching were not in persuasive words of wisdom, but in demonstration of the Spirit and of power . . ."

Younger men in our meetings may feel that they are too young or too spiritually immature to stand up and lead out. Yet, in 1 Timothy 4:12, Paul exhorts Timothy, "Let no one look down on your youthfulness, but rather in speech, conduct, love, faith and purity, show yourself an example of those who believe." Of course, this verse and those that follow it imply that Timothy was a young man who was very serious about the things of God. But a young man doesn't have to have "arrived" spiritually to be fit to share in the Lord's Supper. Like all the rest of us, he's hopefully in the process of becoming more and more like Christ. Clarke writes:

> Worship of the Father takes place in the holy intimacy of the divine family circle. His children approach Him with reverent love, from the youngest to the oldest all having access to Him on equal footing.[11]

Moreover, those who start sharing in the Lord's Supper at an early age have more time to develop in the area of public ministry, and should they demonstrate some gift in that area, it will be noticed by the elders and likely encouraged by them in other venues. Furthermore, anyone who has read the history of the Brethren assembly movement realizes that the Lord used relatively young men to get it started and developed.

Other men may share infrequently because they don't want to take away the opportunity for someone else who might like to participate vocally. While in some respects that's a noble and valid way of reasoning, I would encourage such men to trust the Holy Spirit to lead them as to whether and when they should share. After all, it's very possible that the Holy Spirit has impressed upon you a thought that He's shown to no one else in the meeting on that particular occasion; He's spoken to you especially, and if you don't share it, those present will miss out on the potential blessing. You could even conclude that your refusal to speak up would amount to a limiting or stifling of the Holy Spirit.

As for those men who attend a sizeable assembly as I do (we have around 125 in attendance for the Lord's Supper), the truth is, there's no pressing need for any given man to participate because if he doesn't, he knows someone else will. But as we saw in 1 Corinthians 14, that's not the proper way to look at it. Just like the eager Corinthians, we all need to come prepared to lead out in worship, whether we actually do or not.

Speaking of preparation, Gibbs has some sobering comments to make to us about the fact that the reason many of us don't contribute in the meeting is because many of us come totally unprepared to do so.

> God's word to Israel was: "None shall appear before Me empty" (Exod. 23:15). It is pathetic indeed, at a meeting convened particularly for worship, to see so many who apparently have neither taken the time nor made the effort to put anything in their basket of gratitude. The long periods of silence in many worship meetings are often, not the silences of worshipful adoration, but the silences of spiritual poverty. It will be noted that in Deut. 26 [vv. 1-11], it is individual worship that is in view. It goes without saying, that the quality of our collective worship, will be conditioned by the spirituality of each believer present at the meeting convened for that purpose. The obvious teaching of this passage in Deut. 26 is that each believer should be spiritually exercised during the week, and personally select and arrange his basket of first fruits. He should then bring with him, to the assembly of God's people, a heart filled with his own individual appreciation of all that God is, as revealed in His beloved Son. As each Christian does this, the spiritual tone of the worship meeting will be lifted to a high plane, and God will receive that which He seeks—the worship of His beloved, blood-bought and Spirit-born children. May we not disappoint Him in this![12]

If we're honest with ourselves, this lack of spiritual preparation, maybe even more than fear, is what muzzles many of the men who don't participate audibly in the Lord's Supper. I myself must confess that at times in the past I have not participated in the breaking of bread for this very reason. I may have even spent hours in ministry that week, but I permitted my busyness to deprive me of personal time with the Lord. Consequently, when it came time for the remembrance meeting, I'd feel like I had nothing to offer because I was spiritually dry and would have even felt hypocritical if I'd attempted to contribute to the meeting.

Lastly, when asked what the greatest of all God's commandments is, Jesus reduced those commandments down to two: to love God with everything you have and to love others as you do yourself (Mark 12:28-31). If this characterized the Christian man, would he not be eager to please both God and his fellow believers by his Spirit-led contributions to the Lord's Supper? Could our lack of sacrificial love for God and for our fellow believers be yet another reason why we don't take part audibly in the breaking of bread as we should?

CHAPTER 6

Why or When We Shouldn't Share

As we have just considered, there are a lot of poor excuses for not participating audibly in the Lord's Supper. However, there are some legitimate reasons why we should at times refrain from taking part verbally. The most compelling reason is if we have clearly not been walking with the Lord or living in obedience to His will. I've already made the point that God doesn't expect perfection of those who stand up and take a turn at leading the worship meeting. On the other hand, we must heed and apply to ourselves the very serious warning that the Spirit of God inspired the apostle Paul to issue to the Corinthian church:

> *Therefore whoever eats the bread or drinks the cup of the Lord in an unworthy manner shall be guilty of the body and the blood of the Lord. But a man must examine himself, and in so doing he is to eat of the bread and drink of the cup. For he who eats and drinks, eat and drinks judgment to himself if he does not judge the body rightly. For this reason many among you are weak and sick, and a number sleep. (1 Cor. 11:27-30)*

This passage, of course, is dealing with whether or not a person should even partake of the elements, the bread and the cup, as they pass before him or her. However, if a man is not in the right spiritual condition to take the elements, he is certainly in no position to be standing up and leading the congregation in worship. And what does it mean to be doing these things "in an unworthy manner"? In verses

17-22 of 1 Corinthians 11, it's evident that many of the Corinthian believers were guilty of harboring a divisive spirit, of gluttony, and of selfishness and thoughtlessness toward their fellow believers. Clearly, many other types of inappropriate attitudes and behavior, such as pride or immorality, would fall into this category of conducting oneself in an unworthy manner.

Now, the Lord in His Word does offer us certain remedies for being out of fellowship with Him or with other people. In Matthew 5:23-24, Jesus instructs:

> *"Therefore if you are presenting your offering at the altar, and there remember that your brother has something against you, leave your offering there before the altar and go; first be reconciled to your brother, and then come and present your offering."*

The well-known verse 1 John 1:9 reassures us, "If we confess our sins, He is faithful and righteous to forgive us our sins and to cleanse us from all unrighteousness." Thus the Lord has definitely provided believers with ways to restore fellowship with Him before or as we approach Him in worship so that we don't end up worshiping "in an unworthy manner." It's important, however, that our confessions of sin be genuine and coupled with a determination to leave such sins behind by the power of the Holy Spirit working within us. Consider what God teaches us in Romans 6:1-2, 11-13; 8:12-13:

> *What shall we say then? Are we to continue in sin that grace may increase? May it never be! How shall we who died to sin still live in it? . . . Even so consider yourselves to be dead to sin, but alive to God in Christ Jesus. Therefore do not let sin reign in your mortal body so that you obey its lusts, and do not go on presenting the members of your body to sin as instruments of unrighteousness; but present yourselves to God as those alive from the dead, and your members as instruments of righteousness to God. . . . So then, brethren, we are under obligation, not to the flesh, to live according to the flesh—for if you are living*

> *according to the flesh, you must die; but if by the Spirit you are putting to death the deeds of the body, you will live.*

A situation that pressures some brothers to share in the Lord's Supper has to do with the discomfort they feel when they deem that too long a period of silence has gone by. Personally, I like those periods of silence because they give me more time to meditate on the hymns and Scripture passages that have been offered up to that point in the meeting. Kelly has the right perspective in regard to these periods of silence:

> Again, there may be some outside the assembly, known or unknown, who, out of curiosity, are come to see what the worship is like. Now are you, fearing that they might wonder at the silence from time to time, to read a chapter, or give out some sweet hymn? Need I say that such a step is indefensible, and beneath men who believe in the presence of the Holy Ghost? Some may think there is liberty to do this or the like; but who put such thoughts into the mind? Do you think the Holy Spirit is occupied with what those without may say or think of those within, or anything of the kind? Is He not on the contrary filled with His own thoughts of Christ, and communicating them to us? The becoming thing, therefore, for us to do under such circumstances is to look from ourselves, and those within and without, to God, that He, working by the Spirit, may give us communion with the present thoughts of the Spirit of God about the Lord Jesus Christ.[13]

Of course, Kelly's remarks are primarily concerned with whether our worship and remembrance of the Lord in the breaking of bread is being directed by the Holy Spirit or not. Such a consideration should weigh heavily upon the mind of any man who contemplates participating vocally in the meeting. Indeed, a man may have spent lots of time before the Lord throughout the week and may even have prepared some thoughts to potentially share in the breaking of bread. However, before actually sharing those thoughts, such a man should ask himself if the Spirit is indeed leading him to share at that moment and if what he has to share seems to fit with the direction in which the

Spirit has led the meeting thus far. Let's not wrest away the control of the meeting from the Holy Spirit by forcing upon the meeting a thought, a passage, a hymn, or even a prayer that is not truly Spirit led.

To wrap up this chapter, I'd like to suggest that, normally, a man should not participate in the breaking of bread every week, particularly if his participation tends to be lengthy. Obviously, in a very small assembly, such a guideline may be impossible to follow. However, in an assembly where there are at least ten or more men who could take a vocal part in the meeting and are all willing to do so, those who insist on sharing at length every single week are, without doubt, taking away opportunities for other men to participate. If those other men are somewhat timid, as is often the case, aggressive, every-week participators will even further inhibit those who are hesitant to share. Those times of silence mentioned previously may well give the timid man an opportunity to actually do what the Spirit is prompting him to do—stand up and lead the meeting in worship of the Lord.

CHAPTER 7

What We Should and Shouldn't Share

Anyone who has attended an assembly for any length of time and who has been in regular attendance at the breaking of bread has a good idea of the specific ways in which the men of the assembly will contribute vocally to the meeting. The way that most men are willing to take part publicly is to suggest a hymn or a chorus for the congregation to sing together.

While simple to do, choosing the right song can greatly enhance the spirit of worship within the group. I've noticed that some men have a particular knack for choosing the right hymn at the right time. The song chosen should be one that leads us to remember Christ and His redemptive work or to worship the Father and the Son for who they are. Hymns that focus on exhorting us to live the Christian life, while very important, are not generally appropriate during the remembrance meeting because they distract from the purposes of that meeting. Thus hymns like "Give of Your Best to the Master," "Trust and Obey," "Who Is on the Lord's Side?" or "Sweet Hour of Prayer" would be better used during the traditional preaching meeting or at the midweek prayer meeting.

Hymns such as those found (though not exclusively) in *Hymns of Worship and Remembrance*[14] (the so-called "black book") are typically more in line with what we're striving to do in the Lord's Supper—hymns such as "Hallelujah! What a Savior!" or "The Holy One Who Knew No Sin" certainly focus our attention on Jesus and on all that He is and has done for us. Possibly even better are hymns like "A Thousand, A Thousand Thanksgivings" or "Lord of Glory, We Adore Thee" for the fact that, as we sing those hymns, we are directly addressing those whom we are worshiping. Kelly expresses the same basic thought as to the appropriateness of hymns in the breaking of bread:

> An individual may give out a hymn to be sung in which he delights, and which may be not only beautiful but true and spiritual in itself; but it may be a mistake in him to give it out – a wholly unsuitable hymn for the occasion on which he desires it to be sung.[15]

I feel that here Kelly may be implying not only that a man should not call out a song of exhortation to Christians, but that he should not even call out a hymn of worship, praise, or thanksgiving if it doesn't seem to fit in with the direction in which the Spirit is moving the meeting.

Another common way in which men participate in the Lord's Supper is to read a passage of Scripture with or without comment. It's entirely appropriate to simply read a passage of Scripture without comment, allowing the Scriptures alone to do the talking. This is also something that a man not used to speaking in public could feel more comfortable doing. I would say that, as a rule, a relatively short passage of Scripture should be used, avoiding the reading of whole chapters or jumping from verse to verse to verse throughout the Bible. I think that listeners begin to tune out when a reading goes on too long. Though we're doing what we're doing primarily for God, we need to be considerate of our human audience as well; after all, we're trying to lead and aid them in their worship. Again, while every verse in the Bible is precious, being the very Word of God, passages that deal with how to live the Christian life would typically not be as appropriate as passages that speak of the person and work of the Father or the Son, particularly if such passages are read without comment.

Of course, as most of us have observed, some men will read a Scripture portion and then continue on with some thoughts of their own. On many occasions, such comments have been wonderfully uplifting and enabling to me as I seek to worship the Lord. Those who venture to make such comments tend to be the men in the assembly who have the closest relationships with the Lord and who are most familiar with His Word. They've been reflecting on these matters throughout the week, and even over the years, which is why such words seem to come so easily for them and why the Spirit can so readily use them. This is not to say that a man who is spiritually less mature has nothing worthy to share with the group. Indeed, the young in Christ can often have some very refreshing thoughts to offer in worship, especially if they've been spending regular time with God. For the most part, I would encourage a man to keep his comments on the Scriptures brief. The breaking of bread is not a time for sermons, and obviously, the longer a man talks, the less time and opportunity other men will have to participate.

And speaking of sermons, this meeting is not for the purpose of teaching. That is the function of the meeting often termed "The Family Bible Hour" held on Sunday mornings. In his pamphlet entitled "The Lord's Supper," Harry Ironside makes this very point:

> It is important, first of all, to understand that we do not come together to pray, nor yet to preach, nor sing or listen to teaching, nor to enjoy Christian fellowship. We come together to meet the Lord Himself, to be solely occupied with Him, to offer Him the worship of our hearts, and to remember what He passed through for us. Let me put it this way: Suppose that on a given Lord's Day morning it were known definitely that our Savior, in person, would be present in our church building. How do you think real Christians would act on such an occasion? . . . [We would not] be coming to listen to one preaching or teaching the Word of God. Our one desire would be to see Him, to fix our adoring eyes upon His blessed Face; if we spoke at all, it would be to tell something of His sufferings for us, and the gratitude and worship that would fill our hearts as we recalled the agony He endured on the cross. . . . No one would dare to push Christ aside, and to take His place as the teacher of others, unless requested by the Lord.[16]

Now, of course it's true that as various men stand up, read Bible passages, and make comments about them, a certain amount of teaching will occur; I've learned so much myself about the person and work of the Father and the Son through attendance and attention at many breaking of bread services. Nevertheless, teaching should be a by-product, not the goal, of a man as he stands to lead the meeting in worship.

Yet another valuable way to contribute audibly in the Lord's Supper is to simply offer a short prayer of worship, praise, adoration and/or thanksgiving to the Lord for who He is and what He's done, especially to save us. This seems to be almost a lost art here in the United States, at least, in my experience. Most men who read Scriptures and then make some comments of their own will conclude with prayer, which is quite appropriate. But for some reason, many men seem reluctant to do nothing more than to stand and pray. That's why I found the Lord's Supper in that assembly in the Middle East so refreshing—there was always a major emphasis on prayer in that particular meeting, a spontaneous outpouring of gratitude to their Savior. Again, I emphasize that you don't have to be longwinded or spiritually sophisticated when you pray. The Lord and others listening are touched by simple, heartfelt prayers.

Avoid teaching through your prayers; the Lord doesn't need to learn anything. In his pamphlet, Ironside adds this observation about other inappropriate types of prayer:

> It is also well understood that prayers of a general nature, prayers for the salvation of the lost, and intercessions for the sick are quite out of place. These subjects of prayer are necessary, proper, and good, but should be brought before the Lord at the weekly prayer meeting and in private prayer.[17]

I love the way Gibbs summarizes the concept of prayer in the breaking of bread:

> . . . the worshipper does not ask God for a single thing. He does not come to God with a petition on his lips, but with a present in his hand.[18]

There are some who are fond of sharing a story or event from their own lives or the lives of others. Such testimonies can be inspirational and can genuinely add to the meeting if they are used to demonstrate the greatness and glory of God or one's growth in understanding and appreciation of what Jesus has done to redeem us. The danger of a testimony or a story, however, is that the focus can often be more on the person in the story than on the Lord Himself—too much on "me" and not enough on "Him." Along the same lines, the breaking of bread is not the place for a man to stand and exhort his listeners to live the Christian life more seriously, to be more fervent in evangelism, prayer, or Bible study, to develop more of a burden for missions, or anything of the sort.

Less frequently, I have seen other forms of participation in the Lord's Supper that effectively aided the group in their worship and remembrance of Christ. Instead of having the group sing a hymn or chorus, a man will simply read the words of the song slowly and emphatically, inviting his listeners to reflect upon those words. Or he might choose to use a Scripture passage or hymn as a responsive reading, actively engaging the rest of the congregation. Additionally, a participant might share a Christ-centered poem or an excerpt from a book he's reading that leads his fellow-worshipers to give glory to God. Undoubtedly, many of you have experienced yet other ways of leading out in worship that have been appropriate and effective.

CHAPTER 8

A Few Words About Delivery

What? You're going to talk about *delivery?* I thought you just said that this is not about giving a sermon! I thought that our participation was primarily to please God, not men! Yet we must remember that the Lord's Supper is a public meeting. Any audible participation must, therefore, also be for the edification of the listeners and the enhancement of their worship.

First of all, let me make it clear that those who participate verbally in the Lord's Supper don't have to be polished and sophisticated in the delivery of what they say. It's understood that a man young in the faith or one who has limited experience speaking before a group of people is not going to be as eloquent as one who has shared in the meeting for many years. Nevertheless, there are a few simple measures that any man can take to assure that his sharing is of the utmost benefit to the worshipers as a whole.

I'll say again that I think it's very important in most cases to keep your participation fairly brief. Normally, five minutes or less is plenty for any one man to participate, especially in a meeting that lasts no more than an hour and in which there are a number of brothers who could take part. In general, have the mentality of giving way to others whom the Spirit may want to speak through as well. I distinctly recall an occasion when a man stood up in our remembrance meeting and proceeded to share for probably ten to fifteen minutes, turning to a dozen or more Scripture passages in rapid-fire succession. Long before he was done he had lost me, as I was so distracted by the messenger that I couldn't focus on his message.

When you do speak, you should stand and speak loudly, clearly, and somewhat deliberately. It is very annoying to those listening if they have to strain to hear what is being said. We've probably all seen men stand up and proceed to mumble through what they had to say or to speak with a voice that only those immediately around them could hear. As good as such a man's intentions may be, and while his failure to use a public voice may reflect his lack of confidence, he has not contributed to leading the congregation in worship if people can't hear him.

Closely related to the need to speak out is the need to face the majority of those in the meeting. If you are seated near the front of the sanctuary, turn and face the bulk of the audience. If you are sitting on the side, face the middle. One time in our assembly, a young man attending the breaking of bread sat in the very first row of our sanctuary, which seats about 160 people. That day the room was practically full, and there were others sitting in the foyer at the back of the room. The young man stood up and shared at some length but continued to face the front with his back to everyone present. Now, I would imagine that his desire was to be humble and not draw attention to himself, which I respect. Nevertheless, when you speak in any public context, you *will* draw attention to yourself; that's unavoidable. You may as well do all that you reasonably can do to be understood. I'm sure that many of the worshipers in attendance that morning could not hear anything the young man had to say and thus were denied the potential blessing of it.

If you're reading a passage of Scripture or a hymn, mention its reference or number, even twice, and then pause for a few seconds to give people (including the pianist!) time to locate that passage in their Bibles or that hymn in their hymnbooks. Finally, for those of us in Western, time-oriented cultures, be aware of the time. If the meeting is almost over and it's time to pass the elements, don't launch into a lengthy commentary on a Scripture portion or give a detailed testimony. Instead, consider doing what's necessary at that juncture in the meeting by praying for the bread or for the cup if the bread has already been circulated.

CHAPTER 9

How to Follow the Leading of the Holy Spirit

Several times in the preceding chapters I have alluded to the idea of the Holy Spirit leading us as we proceed through a breaking of bread service. To many, this concept of the Holy Spirit leading us during the Lord's Supper may seem like a mysterious one. What exactly does "the leading of the Holy Spirit" mean? How precisely does He lead us during the meeting?

Well, let's look at what the Scriptures have to say about this subject. Key passages about the ministry of the Holy Spirit can be found in the gospel of John. There Jesus teaches us, "But the Helper, the Holy Spirit, whom the Father will send in My name, He will teach you all things, and bring to your remembrance all that I said to you" (14:26). Jesus later adds, "When the Helper comes, whom I will send to you from the Father, that is the Spirit of truth who proceeds from the Father, He will testify about Me" (15:26). He continues by saying, "But when He, the Spirit of truth, comes, He will guide you into all the truth. . . . He will glorify Me for He will take of Mine and will disclose it to you" (16:13-14).

Some years later, the Lord through Paul proclaims, ". . . no one can say, 'Jesus is Lord,' except by the Holy Spirit" (1 Cor. 12:3). Paul states in Philippians 3:3 that we "worship in the Spirit of God." In Romans 8:26, he informs us that "the Spirit also helps our weakness; for we do not know how to pray as we should, but the Spirit Himself intercedes for us with groanings too deep for words." Finally, in 1 Corinthians 2:10-13 we are given the following crucial instruction regarding the ministry of the Holy Spirit on our behalf:

> *For to us God revealed them [His wisdom, truth, and blessings] through the Spirit; for the Spirit searches all things, even the depths of God. For who among men knows the thoughts of a man except the spirit of the man which is in him? Even so the thoughts of God no one knows except the Spirit of God. Now we have received, not the spirit of the world, but the Spirit who is from God, so that we may know the things freely given to us by God, which things we also speak, not in words taught by human wisdom, but in those taught by the Spirit, combining spiritual thoughts with spiritual words.*

So, essentially, among the main ministries of the Holy Spirit in our lives are His efforts to bring glory to Jesus and to aid us in our worship of Him, even to the point of reminding us of our Lord's character, teachings, and accomplishments and assisting us when we pray or speak about our God and Savior. Do we then want the Holy Spirit to lead us through the Lord's Supper? Most definitely!

But what about this idea of the breaking of bread having a particular theme? Well, I can't really point to a Scripture verse that teaches that there should be one specific theme in the Lord's Supper, but I can say this—that God is a God of order, not confusion (1 Cor. 14:33, 40). Logically, then, one would expect the Holy Spirit to lead us in a particular direction in our worship as opposed to a random, disjointed collection of our own thoughts, experiences, and selections from the Scriptures and hymnbooks.

In one sense, you could say that the theme of every breaking of bread has already been determined. You could make a case for saying that as long as an individual's contribution moves us to worship God and to remember the redemptive work of Christ on our behalf, he has kept to the basic theme of the Lord's Supper. Nevertheless, I normally find that the worship experience is far more edifying to me when I perceive a consistent theme developing throughout the meeting instead of a series of largely unrelated hymns, Scriptures, prayers, and comments. Common themes that arise include the love of God, His grace and mercy, His righteousness and holiness, His deliverance of us from our sinful state, Jesus' sacrifices for us, the victories and conquests He has achieved, and so on.

However, just as I cannot identify a Scripture passage that says we must pursue a single theme during the breaking of bread, I also cannot produce one that prohibits us from developing more than one theme per meeting. In other words, nowhere do the Scriptures teach that the Holy Spirit is confined to developing a single theme throughout the meeting. Very possibly, He may have more than one point He wants to emphasize. Maybe He wants to bring out several aspects of Jesus' or the Father's person and work in a single meeting.

I think this realization is important because of the fact that many men can be paralyzed by the fear that, if they were to participate, they might not be following the theme exactly. There's liberty to share what the Spirit is burdening you to share, and I've noticed that many of those who participate regularly don't necessarily stick precisely to whatever theme seems to be unfolding. I think it's also important because, if we're convinced that it's imperative to stick to a single theme, we can become overly judgmental of those we view as departing from the theme, and any such judgment of believers by other believers is a very destructive practice.

In reality, following the leading of the Holy Spirit is not as mysterious a concept as it might appear. After all, the Lord has given us ears to hear, a brain to comprehend, and a spirit to respond in worship. If we have come with a single-minded desire to worship, and if we pay close attention to every contribution throughout the meeting, we'll notice the direction in which the Spirit is leading us. And be assured that whatever direction the Spirit leads us in will always be in total agreement with the Word of God.

Specifically, there are a number of ways in which a man can continue the developing theme. For example, he can read or comment on a phrase or verse of a hymn that has already been sung, or he can suggest the singing of another hymn with a message similar to that of the previous hymn. He can make a related comment about a Scripture passage previously read or expounded upon. He can read or comment on another Bible passage that he's reminded of by a hymn, Scripture portion, or prayer already offered. He can offer a prayer based on the words of a hymn or Scripture passage that's been shared. He can relate a personal experience or even a general news event to the developing theme. Again, if a man is attentive and comes prepared to participate in the meeting (the subject of the next chapter), he shouldn't have great difficulty picking up on how the Holy Spirit is leading.

CHAPTER 10

How Best to Prepare to Participate

So how do we get ourselves ready to participate in the Lord's Supper? Without a doubt, the number one way to do so is to walk closely with God, drawing near to Him and spending regular time with Him in the Word and prayer. If you do that, you should have plenty to share. Gibbs wholeheartedly concurs:

> The fire of worship needs the constant renewing of fuel if it is to rise, like the smoke of the morning sacrifice, to God. The fuel needed is the study of, meditation in and obedience to the word of God, plus a life of prayer and devotion. If this fuel is not forthcoming, then the fire of worship on the altar of the soul will die, and God will be denied the worship He seeks. The awkward and poverty-stricken silences that sometimes occur in a gathering of believers for worship is the sad consequence of this particular hindrance of slothfulness. The saints have nothing to give God, because they have not gathered anything from God.[19]

Here, older men, if they are spiritually inclined, usually have an advantage over younger men because they have had much more time to study the Scriptures in depth. Nevertheless, younger men who are so motivated and diligent can actually acquire a fairly good understanding of God's Word in a relatively short period of time, and certainly enough to begin contributing to the Lord's Supper. The more time you spend with the Lord and the better you know His Word, the more often thoughts to share in the meeting will come to you as you sit and listen. Still, it's fine if you want to prepare something to share ahead of time, and likely even better for you if you are unaccustomed to participating in the meeting. In time, you will learn how to tailor what you've prepared to the direction in which the Spirit is taking the meeting.

As I've mentioned previously, it's critical to listen carefully throughout the meeting, attending closely to and reflecting upon every song, prayer, Scripture passage, and comment offered. By doing so, you will more likely ensure that your own contribution ties in with the developing theme as much as possible. Remember, it's not, "What do *I* want to say?" but "What does the *Holy Spirit* want me to say? What does He seem to be focusing our attention on?"

In addition to spending ample time in the Bible, also make note of and familiarize yourself with hymns and choruses that are worshipful and that remember the Lord. That's why in many assemblies we use the hymnbook, *Hymns of Worship and Remembrance*. The older I get, the more I appreciate this powerful collection of hymns, sometimes because of the tunes themselves but much more often because of the spiritual depth of expression of the lyrics.

Of course, there are many other wonderful and appropriate songs in other hymnbooks that could be used. In the assembly I attend, we have another such hymnbook in the pews along with the black book, and both books are frequently used in our observance of the Lord's Supper.

Another way to best prepare for the meeting is to arrive punctually so that you can follow the meeting from the very beginning. This is advice from someone who himself is quite time-challenged but who recognizes the great value of arriving on time. Being punctual means you will be able to pick up on everything the Spirit intends to bring out on that particular occasion. It may also spare you from calling out a hymn that the group has already sung or commenting on a Bible passage in a very similar way to what another brother may have already done. In fact, for that very reason, when I arrive late, I tend to feel somewhat more inhibited about participating vocally. I simply don't know what's gone on up to the point of my arrival.

Even preferable to arriving on time is to arrive a few minutes early. This early arrival would not be for the purpose of getting in a few more minutes of fellowship with other believers. It would be a time to enter the meeting place and sit in silence, preparing oneself to worship. If necessary, it's also a good time to confess sins to the Lord. Of course, this time of personal preparation can begin even earlier, either the night before the meeting or the morning of it before you leave your house. In addition to preparing yourself spiritually, it's wise to prepare yourself physically by getting a good night's sleep before the meeting. That way, you will be alert during the meeting instead of fighting the urge to fall asleep.

A final suggestion that might help a number of people to follow the developing theme of the breaking of bread is to try to jot down brief notes about what's happening as the meeting progresses. When I've done this myself, I have often been amazed at how clear the direction of the meeting becomes.

PART 4
CONCLUSION

NEW TESTAMENT PRIESTS,
Speak Up!

Afterword

You may have wondered whether the training sessions I described earlier made any difference in our assembly. My answer to that would be yes, but not to the degree that I had hoped for. Among my closing comments to the men who participated in those sessions was the thought that, ultimately, each of them must come to the place where pleasing God compels him to spend regular time with the Lord and to overcome his inhibitions against standing and leading out in worship. That's harder for some than for others, but now a couple of men are participating verbally who were not doing so before.

At the very least, I believe all of these men have a better understanding of what the breaking of bread in assembly circles means and why many of those who regularly attend our assembly view that meeting as the one they must be at each week. I'm also convinced that doing whatever we can to persuade believing men to accept the responsibility and enjoy the privilege of serving as priests who lead the congregation in worship is a worthwhile venture. I think most of us are excited and encouraged to hear yet another man, young or older, stand up for the first time and, in sincerity of heart, give honor and praise to his God and Savior, and I'm positive the Lord feels that way as well.

When I consider the assembly that I currently attend, I feel that we are blessed to have a fairly large number of men who are willing to take the lead in our worship meeting. As I think of those men who participate audibly and regularly, no two of them are alike. Each of them has his own "style" of sharing, if you will, and each one contributes to the quality of the worship in his own special way. The meeting is enriched by each man's offering, and it would be both our loss and the Lord's if any of these men stopped making his unique contribution. Of course, how much richer still our worship would be if even more of our men could be persuaded to start participating and adding to our remembrance of Christ in a way that only they can do! May the Lord use what you have just finished reading to encourage this to happen in assemblies throughout this country and beyond.

Addendum A

So What's In It for Women?

You will undoubtedly remember that I came out very clearly against vocal participation in the Lord's Supper by women. Many of those very women might be accustomed to speaking out in the workplace, in other areas of assembly life, or in other venues, expressing their opinions or even leading. Well then, what are women to do week in and week out at the breaking of bread?

Very simply, they should do exactly what men who remain silent during the meeting do, with the single exception of being open to the Spirit's leading them to take part audibly in the meeting. Like the men, they should come spiritually prepared to worship God and to remember His Son. They should come with the expectation that the Spirit will lead all present in a time of worship that will bring pleasure to the Lord. They can meditate on every song that they sing, every prayer that is offered, and every Scripture portion that is shared, and consider in their minds other Bible passages or hymns that might aid them in their worship. Particularly during times of silence throughout the meeting, a woman can spend that time addressing God and the Lord Jesus in worshipful prayer and praise. Like a man, a woman can allow the worship experience of the Lord's Supper to set the tone for the coming week.

I don't deny that it must be challenging to women, especially those who are used to leading in other contexts, to remain silent in the breaking of bread week after week. However, again, I would point out that the silence of women during this meeting does certainly appear to be God's will based on the Scripture passages previously cited.

I would therefore encourage you ladies to focus much more on what you *can* do in the meeting than on what you can't. Remember also that men in the assembly live under certain restrictions themselves. For example, since most of the men are not elders, they are not the primary decision-makers in the congregation and so must learn to submit to the decisions and direction that the elders take as long as they fellowship at that assembly.

Keep in mind as well that these biblical restrictions on women are only temporary and will fall away once we're in heaven. There our sin nature will have been totally eradicated, removing the need for the limitations placed upon women as a result of the fall. The relationship between men and women in heaven will be completely different, as the spiritual hierarchy of men over women that's now in place will give way to an equality of all God's worshipers regardless of gender. And sisters, in the course of eternity, that day is really not very far off!

I myself have sat through many a Lord's Supper in which I was greatly blessed and in which I worshiped the Lord in a meaningful way despite the fact that I didn't utter a single word. May the women be determined to be fully engaged during every breaking of bread and totally resolved to worship the Lord in a way that's just as pleasing to God as that of a man who participates audibly in the meeting.

Addendum B

Session Worksheets

Session 1
Lord's Supper Scriptures

Chapter 1

Session 2
Other Related Scriptures

Chapters 2, 3, & 4

Session 3
Practical Concerns

Chapters 5, 6, & 7

Session 4
Practical Concerns

Chapters 8, 9, & 10

Session 5
Practice

Psalm 103

Ephesians 2:1-10

Hymns:

Session 6
Practice

Bible Passage Evaluation:

Suitable Hymns:

Less Suitable Hymns:

Session 7
Practice

Prayer Contents:

Comments on a Bible Passage:

Comments on a Hymn:

Session 8
Practice

Prayer Contents:

Comments on a Bible Passage:

Comments on a Hymn:

SESSION 9
PRACTICE

Prayer Contents:

Comments on a Bible Passage:

Comments on a Hymn:

Session 10
Practice

Prayer Contents:

Comments on a Bible Passage:

Comments on a Hymn:

Endnotes

1. Kelly, William. *Lectures on the Church of God.* Oak Park, IL: Bible Truth Publishers, 151.
2. Clarke, Arthur G. *New Testament Church Principles.* 3rd ed. Kilmarnock, Scotland: John Ritchie Ltd., 1962, 32.
3. Kelly, William. *Lectures on the Church of God.* Oak Park, IL: Bible Truth Publishers, 156-7.
4. Morris, Leon. *The First Epistle of Paul to the Corinthians: The Tyndale New Testament Commentaries.* Grand Rapids, MI: William B. Eerdmans Publishing Co., 1985, 194.
5. Glock, David A. *Our Reason To Be: The Centrality of the Lord's Supper in the Life of the Assembly.* Dubuque, IA: ECS Ministries, 2003, 22.
6. Gibbs, Alfred P. *Worship: The Christian's Highest Occupation.* 2nd ed. Dubuque, IA: ECS Ministries (Walterick Publishers), 101-102.
7. Ibid, 245.
8. Clarke, Arthur G. *New Testament Church Principles.* 3rd ed. Kilmarnock, Scotland: John Ritchie Ltd., 1962, 45.
9. Glock, David A. *Our Reason To Be: The Centrality of the Lord's Supper in the Life of the Assembly.* Dubuque, IA: ECS Ministries, 2003, 6.
10. Kelly, William. *Lectures on the Church of God.* Oak Park, IL: Bible Truth Publishers, 147.
11. Clarke, Arthur G. *New Testament Church Principles.* 3rd ed. Kilmarnock, Scotland: John Ritchie Ltd., 1962, 42.

[12] Gibbs, Alfred P. *Worship: The Christian's Highest Occupation.* 2nd ed. Dubuque, IA: ECS Ministries (Walterick Publishers), 34-35.

[13] Kelly, William. *Lectures on the Church of God.* Oak Park, IL: Bible Truth Publishers, 146.

[14] *Hymns of Worship and Remembrance.* Dubuque, IA: ECS Ministries (Truth & Praise, Inc).

[15] Kelly, William. *Lectures on the Church of God.* Oak Park, IL: Bible Truth Publishers, 146.

[16] Ironside, Harry A. *The Lord's Supper.* Port Colborne, ON: Gospel Folio Press.

[17] Ibid.

[18] Gibbs, Alfred P. *Worship: The Christian's Highest Occupation.* 2nd ed. Dubuque, IA: ECS Ministries (Walterick Publishers), 37.

[19] Ibid, 224.

About the Author

Mike Stephenson began his spiritual journey while a student at the University of North Carolina, coming to know Christ through the campus ministry of the Navigators. His interest in missions was piqued at an Urbana missions conference. After graduating from college, Mike served with Literature Crusades for two years in South America. Through that experience, he met his wife, Kathy, and he was also introduced to the Brethren assemblies.

After completing additional education back in the USA in Bible, missions, and linguistics (with an emphasis in TESL – teaching English as a second language), Mike and Kathy and their two sons spent the next eight years in the Middle East. There he taught English while they served as tentmaker missionaries, first with Operation Mobilization and then under the auspices of CMML.

More recently, Mike taught missions at Emmaus Bible College while also developing a minor in TESL for the college's Intercultural Studies Department. Currently, Mike and Kathy are back in their home assembly of Plymouth Bible Chapel in Plymouth, Minnesota and are actively serving the Lord there.